My
Pearl

A Young Woman's
Pledge to Purity

K.A. Shows

WestBow
PRESS
A DIVISION OF THOMAS NELSON

ISBN: 978-1-4497-3705-4 (sc)

Library of Congress Control Number: 2012900822

WestBow Press books may be ordered through booksellers or by contacting:

WestBow Press
A Division of Thomas Nelson
1663 Liberty Drive
Bloomington, IN 47403
www.westbowpress.com
1-(866) 928-1240

Printed in the United States of America

WestBow Press rev. date: 2/07/2012

Given To

_____

By

_____

On

_____

My pearl is promised to one.

He is chosen by God.

My pearl is a gift from God.

He loves me as himself.

My pearl is pure.

He lives according
to God's word.

My pearl is of great value.

He sells all he has to have it.

My pearl is worth far more than rubies.

He is confident and
lacks nothing of value.

My pearl is highly favored.

He does what God commands.

My pearl is beautiful.

His eyes have made a covenant
never to look at it lustfully.

My pearl is clean.

He does not trample
it under his feet.

My pearl is clothed in modesty.

He sees the beauty
of my good deeds.

My pearl is old fashioned.

His eyes do not mock.

My pearl is expensive.

He pays for it on layaway.

My pearl is pleasing to the eye.

He is self-controlled.

My pearl is desirable.

He is filled with a
Godly jealously.

My pearl is a treasure.

He is gentle and
humble in heart.

My pearl reflects the faces of men.

His eyes are good.

My pearl is an inheritance.

He seeks my father's
blessing.

My pearl is a legacy.

He will give it to my children.

My pearl is delicate.

He is careful to do what is right in the eyes of the Lord.

My pearl is guarded.

He is a watchman on the wall.

My pearl is safe in a high tower.

He is filled with peace.

My pearl was birthed from
the smallest seed.

His faith can move mountains.

My pearl was baptized with water.

He lives by the Spirit and
keeps in step with the Spirit.

My pearl has a name.

He professes Jesus is Lord.

My pearl has a purpose.

His offspring will be Godly.

My pearl is a witness.

He walks in truth
and freedom.

My pearl is a parable.

He desires the secrets
of heaven.

My pearl is a covenant.

He is mindful.

My pearl is blessed.

He is full of praise.

My pearl is holy and dearly loved.

His eyes are full of grace.

My Pledge to Purity

Because I am God's precious daughter, I pledge to keep myself physically and emotionally pure prior to my marriage. I will trust my heavenly Father to provide abundantly the self-control, wisdom, patience and courage I will need. I promise to keep my dating relationships open before God and my parents, seeking their council from the beginning.

My Prayer for Purity Restored

Father, I thank You that You are faithful to remove the shame of impurity from me. I accept Your forgiveness, and by Your Grace, I release myself, my partner(s), my parents, my perpetrator(s) from blame and judgement. I thank You, Father, that You have washed me clean inside and out with Jesus' blood and, as Your beautiful daughter, I am free to live a pure and holy life once again.

People Who Have
Pledged to Help Me

Promises God has Made
to Me in His Word